Leader's GUIDE

for use with

TRIUMPH OVER TEMPTATION

Encounters at the Testing Tree

by

Jonathan Underwood

STANDARD PUBLISHING

Cincinnati, Ohio 39977

ISBN 0-87239-790-4

Contents

Foreword 5

Six-week Study 7
- Lesson 1 8
- Lesson 2 10
- Lesson 3 12
- Lesson 4 14
- Lesson 5 16
- Lesson 6 18

Thirteen-week Study 21
- Lesson 1 22
- Lesson 2 24
- Lesson 3 26
- Lesson 4 28
- Lesson 5 30
- Lesson 6 32
- Lesson 7 34
- Lesson 8 36
- Lesson 9 38
- Lesson 10 40
- Lesson 11 42
- Lesson 12 44
- Lesson 13 46

Foreword

This Leader's Guide is designed to help you lead a group study of Ward Patterson's book, *Triumph Over Temptation: Encounters at the Testing Tree*. The book is valuable for study in a variety of settings for youth and adults alike.

Perhaps you'd like to use it for a special series in youth meetings or during a mid-week study hour. As such, the six-week course (pages 7-19) would work easily. If you'd like it to fill a quarter's Sunday-school sessions, the thirteen-week course outlined in this guide (pages 21-47) will allow you to spend that time well.

As another option for the Sunday-school hour, the study of this book combined with another study might profit your class. Knofel Staton's book *Discovering My Gifts for Service* (#39978; Leader's Guide, #39979) contains seven chapters of valuable insights for helping Christians discern how God can use them in the church. The two books together contain thirteen chapters, one for each week of a Sunday-school quarter. Staton also has written *Check Your Homelife* (#39973; Leader's Guide, #39963), a nineteen-chapter study of the family. A study of that book combined with a study of Patterson's book would last twenty-five weeks, only one week short of two complete quarters. Perhaps your Sunday-school sometimes does not meet because of a special program, or perhaps you'd like a week just to review. The twenty-five lesson series might be just what you need.

Patterson's book was originally titled *At the Testing Tree* (©1978, The Standard Publishing Company), for which a leader's guide was prepared by Virginia Beddow and John Butler. That material has been adapted and included in this guide. Our thanks to those capable educators.

Six-Week Study

LESSON ONE

Objectives: The group should be able to
1. Outline Satan's approach to Eve.
2. Explain the existence of the original testing tree.
3. Analyze and explain why and how they have been tempted successfully in the past.

Step One: Getting Started
1. Gather several old magazines that have plenty of pictures and advertising. Add construction paper, paste, and scissors. Let the group make montages of things that test or tempt people (could be an individual or small group activity). Be sure to save these montages for future class sessions.
2. Make up a true/false quiz about tempting and testing. Sample statements:
   ____a. Some temptations have no way of escape.
   ____b. Satan tempted Adam directly.
   ____c. Sometimes Satan disguises himself as an angel of light.
   ____d. Each person must accept responsibility for his own sin.
   ____e. Temptation is evil.

Step Two: Digging Deeper
1. Ask the class members to work individually or in small groups to outline the step-by-step development of Satan's approach to Eve, and her weakening responses culminating in sin (Genesis 3:1-6).
   Sample: Genesis 3:
   3:1. Satan introduces doubt—points Eve away from what she has to what is forbidden.
   2. Eve gives a "straight" answer of God's generosity.
   3. Eve mentions the exception to the rule in verse two—there is a tree she cannot even touch.
   4. Satan gives the big lie—flatly contradicts God.
   5. Satan tells Eve what she wishes were true about the tree—that the fruit will make her more like God—that it will impart special knowledge.

6. a. Physical aspects of the fruit match her newfound desires:
   (1) Sensual pleasure—"good for food," "pleasing to the eyes."
   (2) Power and a feeling of superiority—"desirable to make one wise."
   b. She makes Adam a partner in sin. (She becomes an advocate of sin.)
2. Have the class read the preface to *Triumph Over Temptation.*

Step Three: Discussion

1. From reading the preface, discuss: If you were to view temptation as a God-given opportunity to test (and demonstrate) your righteousness, would you act any differently? How?
2. Using the outlines made during the last section, analyze where Eve made her mistakes. How could she have resisted at each of those points?
3. How would you answer someone who asked, "If God is good and loving, why did He put such a tree in the garden?"
4. Contrast the reaction of Abraham to his test in Genesis 22 with Eve's reaction in Genesis 3.

Step Four: Application

Have each member share an experience in temptation, share the points at which he made mistakes, and tell how he could have resisted at each of those points. (A here-and-now practical application of Step Two.)

Also give the class a chance to share some victories in temptation. This will help you close the session on a positive note.

Step Five: Assignments

Read the first two chapters of *Triumph Over Temptation.* (After this, the assignment will be one chapter per week.)

LESSON TWO

Objectives: During the session the group members will

1. Contrast the ways God and Satan work in a temptation/testing situation.
2. Discover the key point at which each of the heroes of the faith in Hebrews 11 resisted temptation.
3. Discuss the meaning of man's testing God.
4. Apply the principles learned by dealing with a case study (see below).

Step One: Getting Started

Formulate and tell a story about an adult (or young adult, depending on the group) facing a temptation. Stop at the point at which the person must make a decision. (In step three, the story will be picked up again.) You might find several story models in Charles Sheldon's *In His Steps*, or back issues of *Straight* magazine.

OR—Have someone pretend to be Isaac. He will relate his experience on Mount Moriah to the class and tell what he learned about temptation and trusting God. (Using a visitor and full costume can make this a very effective presentation.)

Step Two: Digging Deeper

1. In chapter two, the author demonstrates the ways God and Satan work in a temptation/testing situation. Be able to contrast these two methods of operation (God's and Satan's), and study the Scripture passages the author suggests.
2. Assign various Old Testament figures mentioned in Hebrews 11 to small groups for study (e.g., Abel, Noah, Abraham, Isaac, Jacob, Joseph, Moses' parents, Moses, Rahab, Gideon, David, Samuel). Each group will find a testing situation in its Old Testament model's life, and determine the key point within the testing situation that assured victory.

Step Three: Discussion

1. Suppose you are Cain. God has found your offering unaccept

able and has issued the challenge of Genesis 4:7. How would you respond? How would you "master" sin?

2. Patterson says Noah "staked his life on his faith in God." In what ways do we stake our lives on our faith?
3. Abraham did not actually offer his son, but the wording of Hebrews 11:17 sounds as if he did. Patterson explains, "In his mind and in his will and in his intent, he did." Are we sometimes guilty of sin because we have done it in our minds and in our wills and in our intents—even if we don't actually commit the act? At what point does temptation become sin?
4. Joshua and Caleb took a stand for God when the other ten spies said their situation was hopeless. How often do we take a stand for God against such odds? What were some situations that called for such a stand? How can a Christian take his stand in those situations?
5. What do you think it means to "test God"? Have you ever tested Him?

Step Four: Application

Refer to the story from Step One and assign two groups. One group should figure out possible actions and consequences of the testing situation if the person chose Satan's urgings in the situation. The other group should describe the outcome if the person had chosen God's way instead.

If you did not use the story in Step One, have the class suggest two or three temptation situations common to them and suggest positive responses to each.

LESSON THREE

Objectives: The group should be able to

1. Defend the position that Jesus experienced temptation just as we do.
2. Study Jesus' method of responding to the temptation of sin.
3. Utilize Jesus' method in a typical temptation situation.

Step One: Getting Started

Present this problem to the class: A doubter says, "Jesus didn't really experience temptation as we do; He was the Son of God." How would you answer that person? Discuss.

Step Two: Digging Deeper

Read Matthew 4:1-11 or Luke 4:1-13 (Jesus' temptations in the wilderness). Or ask a good reader from the group to do it. The rest of the group should be listening for the method Jesus used to defeat Satan. They may want to take notes during the reading. When the reading is completed, discuss Jesus' method, outlining it on a chalkboard or overhead projector.

Step Three: Discussion

1. Which of the three cited temptations of Jesus do you think was strongest? Why?
2. Angels came and ministered to Jesus after His temptation in the wilderness (Matthew 4:11). What role, if any, do angels play in temptation today?
3. Do you think there is any correlation between the disciples' sleeping in the garden—instead of praying—and their desertion of Jesus when He was arrested? If so, explain.
4. What does it mean that Jesus was tempted in all points, "yet without sin"? *(Leader: note Step Two of Lesson Six in the thirteen-week format.)*

Step Four: Application

Ask the group to suggest and describe a tempting situation.

(You may want to formulate one or two of your own before the lesson, in case participation is low.)

Have various members role play possible responses to the situation, particularly, responses such as Jesus might have given. After the first role play, the group should discuss the portrayal. Then choose another drama team to portray the situation again, based upon what may have been learned in the discussion.

Step Five: Assignment

Read chapter four of *Triumph Over Temptation.*

LESSON FOUR

Objectives: During the session, the group should be able to

1. Name and describe the appropriate defense against each of Satan's three attack points.
2. Clarify the application of those defenses for their own lives by discovering the reappearance of the two triads throughout Scripture.
3. Clarify the application by demonstrating the two triads' relationships to our own contemporary testing situations.

Step One: Getting Started

Have the group read Galatians 5:19-21. Then divide into three groups, corresponding to the three elements of the "tragic triad." Each group should then study Galatians 5:19-21 together and list the sins mentioned in the text that correspond to their particular side of the triad. You may want to have some dictionaries and several different Bible versions on hand to help. Here is a sample of the results of their work:

1. Lust of the flesh—immorality, impurity, sensuality, drunkenness, carousings.
2. Lust of the eyes—idolatry, sorcery, enmities, strife, jealousy.
3. Boastful pride of life—outbursts of anger, disputes, dissensions, factions, envyings.

Step Two: Digging Deeper

Assign the following verses to individual members of the group. From studying the text, they should be able to discern:
the tragic triad (or parts thereof) in
Romans 13:12-14; Galatians 5:24-26; Romans 16:8;
Ephesians 4:31, 32; Ephesians 5:3, 4
the triumphant triad in
1 Thessalonians 5:8; Galatians 5:5, 6; 2 Timothy 1:12, 13;
Ephesians 3:13-19; Romans 8:28
both triads in
Titus 3:3-7; 2 Timothy 2:22-26

Step Three: Discussion

1. What types of sin can you think of that cannot be classified as lust of the flesh, lust of the eyes, or boastful pride of life? Is 1 John 2:16 intended as a summary of all types of sin?
2. How is sanctification related to the triumphant triad?
3. Do you think the Father, Son, and Holy Spirit play different roles corresponding to love, faith, and hope? If so, what? If not, why don't you think so?
4. How are faith, hope, and love related to Christ and the Bible?
5. What is *grace*? What is its role in our defense against temptation?

Step Four: Application

1. Give the montages (Session One) back to the individuals or groups who made them.
   a. The individuals or groups should be able to identify which symbols in the montage correspond to which parts of the tragic triad.
   b. Then the group members should be able to describe how faith, hope, and/or love could defend against the temptations mentioned in 1a.
2. Retrieve the temptation situation stories and dramas mentioned in Session Three. Identify the fronts of spiritual combat in these situations as you did in Application 1.

Step Five: Assignments

1. Read chapter five of *Triumph Over Temptation.*
2. Keep a diary of temptations and tests this week, and of their outcomes.
3. Have a group member research and report on the various interpretations of 1 John 5:16-18.

LESSON FIVE

Objectives: By the end of the session the group members will be able to

1. Name the parts of the armor of God, be able to describe them, and relate them to the true functions of salvation, truth, righteousness, the gospel, faith, and the Word of God.
2. Understand the point at which salvation and forgiveness can turn to apostasy and condemnation.

Step One: Getting Started

Read Paul's statement of conflict from a modern paraphrase or free translation (Romans 7:14-25). Encourage discussion among the group: let them offer personal illustrations of the conflict between intentions and behavior.

Step Two: Digging Deeper

1. Have the group member who researched the various interpretations of 1 John 5:16-18 give his report to the group.
2. Divide the group in half. One half is to study the security of God's salvation as shown in John 15:5; 10:27-29; Romans 3:22-28; 5:1, 2; 8:31-39; 1 John 1:8-10. The other half is to research the conditions under which a Christian may lose his relationship to God (and his salvation)—John 15:2; 1 Corinthians 9:27; 2 Thessalonians 2:3; 1 Timothy 4:1; 2 Timothy 4:3, 4; Hebrews 6:4-8; 10:26; 1 John 3:4-10.
3. When the groups are finished, bring them back together. Each group should summarize its findings to the other half of the class. Then the class should discuss the line between salvation and apostasy. At what point does a person cease to be a Christian? At what point does a person, therefore, lose his salvation? What is the difference between a Christian who sins and is forgiven, and a Christian who departs from the faith and then loses his salvation?

Step Three: Discussion

1. Is it possible to wear part of, but not the "whole armor of God"? Why or why not?

2. Discuss the offensive and defensive qualities of each piece of the whole armor of God:
   Breastplate
   Belt
   Sandals
   Shield
   Helmet
   Sword
3. How is "putting on Christ" similar to wearing "the whole armor of God"?
4. Harmonize 1 John 5:16 with 1 John 5:18.
5. What is "sin leading to death"?
6. How do you know whether a person is guilty of "sin leading to death"? How much right do you think humans have to make such a judgment?

Step Four: Application

Have the group share their temptation/testing diaries from last week. Discuss:

a. How did the defeat or victory depend on faith, hope, and/or love?
b. How did the armor of God help in the testing situations? (Or, how could the armor have helped?)

Step Five: Assignments

1. Read chapter six.
2. Divide the "Texts for Tests" references in the appendix following chapter six among the group to read and summarize for the last class session.

LESSON SIX

Objectives: The group should be able to

1. Explain why we should not pray for temptation.
2. Enumerate plans for applying in their personal lives the truths learned during this mini-course.

Step One: Getting Started

Have the group members recount and explain their assigned verses from "Texts for Tests" to the rest of the class.

Step Two: Digging Deeper

Patterson lists several lessons we can learn from Hebrews 12. Ask the group to compare Patterson's list with the lessons they learned from their research assignment reported above. Note any of the texts for tests that support the lessons from Hebrews 12:

1. Be conscious of the greats of the past (12:1).
2. Rid yourselves of all encumbrances and run wisely (12:1).
3. Put your difficulties in perspective (12:4).
4. Remember the Fatherhood of God (12:5-11).
5. Have courage! Encourage others (12:12, 13).
6. Run the race of peace and holiness (12:14).
7. Keep up with the grace of God (12:18).
8. Don't get tripped up by the roots of worldliness (12:15).
9. Watch out for the sensual (12:16).

Step Three: Discussion

1. How do you feel about temptation in light of the fact that we possess the power of God within us (2 Corinthians 4:7)?
2. What reasoning does the author give for not praying for tests and temptations? How do you respond to his reasoning?
3. In what sense might we say that praying for temptation is testing God?
4. Patterson says, "We live at a critical moment." What's critical about it?
5. How does helping others help oneself?

Step Four: Application

To review and summarize ways that a Christian can turn testing into triumph, ask each person to share the one suggestion from the course that has meant the most to him in resisting temptation.

Then have each student write a specific action he will take based on that meaningful suggestion.

Step Five: Closing Projects

List these suggestions in order to turn the information received in this course into dynamic power to live a righteous life. Let the group members respond to the degree that they choose, but challenge them to follow through with the information they have gained in the course.

1. Make a memory project of the Bible verses mentioned in the course that are most useful in overcoming temptation and trials. The persons choosing this project might work out an accountability time schedule for memorizing the verses.
2. Continue the temptation/testing diary as described from the assignment in Session Four.
3. Plan a way or ways to share the concepts learned with the rest of the congregation. For instance, artwork could be displayed occasionally on the church bulletin boards; mini-dramas or plays could be written and staged for a congregational service or assembly; the group could work up a whole program or church service on the topic and share it with the congregation.

Thirteen-Week Study

LESSON ONE

Objectives: The group should be able to
1. Define temptation.
2. State at least one positive potential in temptation.

Step One: Getting Started

As the students arrive, ask them to respond to the following agree/disagree statements. These may be posted, as on the chalkboard, or they may be reproduced so that each student gets a copy.

	Agree	Disagree
1. Temptation has one purpose—to make us sin.	________	________
2. "Count it all joy when ye fall into divers temptations" is a poor translation of James 1:2.	________	________
3. Trials, tests, and temptations may all be the same.	________	________
4. Temptation has possibilities for holiness as well as sinfulness.	________	________

Step Two: Digging Deeper

After the class has had a chance to respond—without discussion—ask them to read the preface to *Triumph Over Temptation*. Allow five to ten minutes. Then ask them to look back over the agree/disagree statements. Discuss each one with the class and try to come to a consensus on each statement.

Display the chart at the end of this lesson on the chalkboard or with the overhead projector. Assign an individual or a small group to look up each Scripture. Then fill in the chart as each student or group reports.

Step Three: Discussion

1. Suppose you were Abraham. How do you think you would have felt when God commanded you to sacrifice Isaac? How would you have settled the conflict of God's promise and His command?

2. Have you ever thought of Israel's wars as tests for its kings? What should the kings have learned from such tests?

Step Four: Application

Have the class review the temptation situations already considered. Together, attempt to list the similarities in the situations as well as some positive potentials that seem to be common to most or all of them. What clues can you list to help identify the potential in a temptation situation before it's too late?

Step Five: Assignment

Read chapter one of *Triumph Over Temptation.*

Chart for Step Two:

Text	Whom Tempted	Victory	Defeat	Lessons Learned
Genesis 3				
Genesis 22				
Deuteronomy 8:2-6				
Job 1:12-22				
Matthew 4:1-11				
Luke 22:31, 32				

LESSON TWO

Objectives: The group should be able to

1. Explain the design of the tree of knowledge of good and evil.
2. Outline Satan's approach to Eve.
3. Explain how God "knows" evil.

Step One: Getting Started

As the students arrive, present them with this problem, "Why was there a tree capable of producing evil in the garden of Eden?" Have them discuss the problem in pairs for a few minutes; then discuss it in the whole class. Be sure to note Patterson's answer on page 14.

Step Two: Digging Deeper

Divide the class into four groups. The first group will look up the following Scriptures and formulate a statement on free will.

Deuteronomy 30:19

Joshua 24:15

1 Kings 18:21

The second and third groups will be the prosecution and the defense for the following "court case": The prosecution will charge that God is responsible for the fall of man because He placed the forbidden fruit in the garden. The defense will seek to exonerate Him.

The fourth group will look at Genesis 3:5, 22, as well as any other Scriptures they find helpful, and explain in what sense Adam and Eve became "like God, knowing good and evil," and why that is not desirable.

Have each group report. Then assign each group to look at Genesis 3 and outline Satan's approach to Eve. Write the outline on the chalkboard as the whole class reports.

Step Three: Discussion

1. Do you ever wish you didn't have free will? Why or why not?
2. What in Satan's approach to Eve do you think was the clincher—the tactic that Eve found most difficult to resist? What is hardest for you to resist?

3. How can you tell truth from half-truth?
4. Read Stedman's explanation of how God knows sin (p.17). In what ways do we sometimes relate moral issues to ourselves rather than to God?
5. When we begin to "want to believe what Satan says," have we already sinned in our hearts? Why or why not?

Step Four: Application

Look back at your outline of Satan's approach to Eve. Have the students imagine a contemporary temptation situation—one that they are likely to face—and compare it with the outline. Note points of similarity.

Then have them note how each point can be resisted. Ask them to observe which areas are hardest for them to resist and to formulate a plan for strengthening their resistance.

Step Five: Assignment

Read chapter one of *Triumph Over Temptation* again.

LESSON THREE

Objectives: The group should be able to
1. Cite the consequences of Adam and Eve's sin.
2. List some positive results of conquering temptation.
3. Explain the gracious nature of the so-called curse on Adam and Eve.

Step One: Getting Started

Duplicate the following sentence fragments. Give a copy to each student as he arrives and ask him to complete them.

1. If Adam had taken his responsibility as a husband,
2. When I get caught in sin,
3. Temptation can serve an ennobling purpose if
4. If Adam and Eve had stayed in the garden,

Have some or all of the students share their responses, but limit discussion at this point.

Step Two: Digging Deeper

Read Genesis 3:6-24. List the following headings on the chalkboard and have the class list consequences of Adam and Eve's sin under each.

Self-image
Spiritual relationships
Family relationships
Ecological relationships

When God walked in the garden in the cool of the day, He called to Adam, but Adam hid. Have the class write how that encounter might have been if Adam and Eve had resisted Satan.

Step Three: Discussion

Discuss the sentence fragments from Step One and as many of the questions below as seems appropriate.
1. Why do you think Adam joined his wife in sin?
2. Patterson says Adam looked at sin too casually. How do we today sometimes look at sin too casually? List some areas where this is true.

3. Why do you think Adam and Eve tried to cast blame when God questioned them? In what way does blaming someone else ease our own sense of guilt?
4. Does God "curse" us when we sin? Explain the "curses" on Adam and Eve. What positive features can you find in them?
5. Patterson says pain, submission, toil, and death "are primary testing points in the lives of each of us." Do you agree? Why or why not?

Step Four: Application

Have the class refer back to your discussion of #2 above. Perhaps you will have listed on the chalkboard the areas in which sin is taken casually. Discuss some ways the class—as a whole or individually—can change some of that. Think of ways to increase the sin awareness of individuals, the church, and the community. Then have each student write a plan of action for taking sin seriously in his own life.

Then have them consider the testing points of pain, submission, toil, and death. How would/do the students face these situations? How should they? What positive results should they seek?

Step Five: Assignment

Read chapter two of *Triumph Over Temptation.*

LESSON FOUR

Objectives: The group should be able to
1. Explain the two ways that are open to us in temptation.
2. Defend a position on the question, "Is faith rational?"
3. Make a statement of trust in God.

Step One: Getting Started

List the names of Cain, Noah, Abraham, Joseph, and Moses where the class can see them upon arrival. Ask the students to write the name of the person on this list with whom they most easily identify regarding temptation. Also, have them write the name of the one from whom they have learned the most about conquering temptation.

After they have done this, ask them to find one other person with the same answer to the first question and share their reasons for identifying with that person. Then have them find another person who agrees on the second. They will share the lessons they have learned.

Step Two: Digging Deeper

Divide the class into two groups. The first group will research Genesis 4:3-16 and answer the following questions:
1. Cain faced a choice between two ways. What were they?
2. How could Cain have mastered sin?
3. Why did Cain kill his brother?
4. What does Cain's expression, "Am I my brother's keeper?" say about his priorities?

The second group will research Hebrews 11:6-29 and answer these questions:
1. Explain the nature of the tests faced by Noah, Abraham, Joseph, and Moses.
2. How were these able to triumph in their tests?
3. What statements did any of these make that indicate their priorities?

When the groups report, you should see a stark contrast between Cain, who failed his test, and the others, who were triumphant. Note Patterson's discussion of these situations in the first half of chapter 2 (pages 25ff.).

Step Three: Discussion

1. Why do you think Cain's sacrifice was rejected?
2. What do you think Isaac thought about Abraham's faith? How would you have felt?
3. Consider Joseph. He was sold by his brothers, framed by his master's wife, and forgotten by his companion from prison. How do you suppose he kept his perspective? How do you keep your perspective when everything seems to go wrong?
4. Once Moses fled Egypt in fear. Later, "by faith he left Egypt [leading the whole nation of Israel], not fearing the wrath of the king" (Hebrews 11:27). What do you think made the difference?
5. Discuss the activity from Step One with the entire class.

Step Four: Application

Have the class write a brief skit based on Noah's test. The setting should be contemporary, however, with a specific Scriptural command at stake rather than a special revelation from God such as Noah received. The skit will illustrate how one man or family can take a stand for God in face of opposition, ridicule, or whatever the class includes in the script.

You might want to perform the skit some Sunday evening.

Step Five: Assignment

Read chapter 2 of *Triumph Over Temptation* again.

LESSON FIVE

Objectives: The group should be able to
1. Define the concept of "testing God."
2. Warn someone of the danger of asking for signs from God.

Step One: Getting Started

Post two sheets of posterboard on the wall. Label one TRUST, the other TEST. As the students arrive, give each a small piece of paper (such as a 3 x 5 card) with a name and a Scripture written on it. Each student looks up the Scripture and decides whether the person trusted or tested God. He then attaches his card to the proper poster. (Provide Plasti-Tak or tape.)

Here are some names and Scriptures:

Abraham—Genesis 22:1-19	Abraham—Genesis 20:1-11
Caleb—Numbers 13:25-33	Israel—Exodus 17:1-7
Jacob—Genesis 28:10-22	Moses—Numbers 20:2-13; Deuteronomy 32:48-51
Moses—Exodus 14:10-28	Gideon—Judges 6:36-40
Centurion—Luke 7:1-10	Scribes and Pharisees—Matthew 12:38-42

The names in the left-hand column should be placed under TRUST. Even Jacob—though he seems to some to be making a deal with God—trusted God. He began serving God immediately. He did not wait for God to accomplish all He promised.

The names on the right should be placed under TEST. Even Gideon, as much as he trusted God later, shows a weakness of faith in the test of the fleece.

Step Two: Digging Deeper

Refer to the example of the scribes and Pharisees in Matthew 12:38. This is not an isolated incident. Have the class look up the following Scriptures and write a statement expressing how God feels about our asking for signs. This activity may be done individually or in small groups.

Matthew 16:1-4
Mark 8:11, 12

Luke 11:14-16; 29-32
1 Corinthians 1:18-25

Testing God [Jesus] and asking for a sign are several times equated. It seems to be a matter of a lack of faith to do so. Jesus calls those who ask for signs "an evil and adulterous generation." Patterson says, "We ask Him to prove himself to us rather than accepting Him on the basis of what He has already done."

Step Three: Discussion

1. Why do you think the Israelites continually tested God? Why couldn't they learn their lesson?
2. Patterson says, "Man's *failure at the testing place* is the same thing as man's *testing God*." Do you agree? Why or why not?
3. If it is improper to test God, how or why was Jesus tested (i.e., tempted)? Is there more to a test than refining and improving something? If so, what?
4. Why do you think Peter said Ananias and Sapphira had "tested" God (Acts 5)?
5. Why do you think God did not require David and Bathsheba be stoned for their adultery (cf. Deuteronomy 22:22)? What consequences did they suffer?

Step Four: Application

Patterson says, "Testing God involves doubting God, rebelling against God, grieving God, forgetting God, disobeying God, disbelieving God, ignoring God, hardening the heart against God, following evil cravings, speaking against the ways of God, being ignorant of God's ways, straying from God's path, and being deceived by sin." Have the class suggest at least five contemporary situations that "test God" in one or more of these criteria. Then have them suggest countermeasures to trust God in the same situations.

Step Five: Assignment

Read chapter 3 of the *Triumph Over Temptation.*

LESSON SIX

Objectives: The group should be able to

1. Explain the nature of Jesus' temptations in the wilderness.
2. Relate Jesus' victory over temptation to contemporary testing situations.
3. Give two explanations of Hebrews 4:15.

Step One: Getting Started

As your students arrive, distribute the following agree/disagree statements and ask them to respond.

	Agree	Disagree
1. Satan tried to tempt Jesus, but there was no appeal to Jesus in what Satan suggested.	________	________
2. Jesus was tempted even more than we are because He was God.	________	________
3. Satan led Jesus into temptation, but Jesus was victorious.	________	________
4. Satan tempted Jesus in the areas we might expect Him to be most vulnerable.	________	________

Step Two: Digging Deeper

Have the class research Luke 4:1-13 to see why Jesus' temptations were real. Work together to complete a chart like the one below. Fill in only the Scripture and the Temptation columns before class—let the group fill in the rest.

JESUS' TEMPTATIONS

Scripture	Temptation	Appeal of Temptation	Nature of Temptation
Luke 4:1-4	Turn Stone To Bread	Hunger/Lust of the Flesh	Doubt God's Provision
Luke 4:5-8	Worship Satan to Receive Worldly Glory	Lust of the Eye	Easy Way to Become "Lord of All"
Luke 4:9-13	Jump from Pinnacle	Pride of Life	Get People's Attention/ A Sign of His Messiahship

Step Three: Discussion

Notice, under the "Appeal of the Temptation" column, the three aspects already noted from 1 John 2:16. This seems to summarize the manner in which Jesus was tempted "in all points," as affirmed in Hebrews 4:15. Ask the class what the last part of Hebrews 4:15 means.

You will probably get this answer. "It means that Jesus never sinned, even though He was tempted." There is another explanation, however. Jesus was "tempted in all things . . . yet without sin." He was tempted in all the ways we are with one exception: sin. Our past sin becomes a temptation for us. Sin is habit-forming. But Jesus never failed in temptation. Thus, He had no past sin to tempt Him.

Discuss whether this means He faced less temptation than we. Actually, He faced more. Note Patterson's remarks in the opening paragraph of this chapter. We cave in too easily. That's why our past sin tempts us. Jesus "bore all that Satan could bring to bear on Him." And He won!

Step Four: Application

Go back to the chart you made in Step Two. Add another column: solution. Notice how Jesus overcame each temptation. Then divide the class into three groups. Each will examine one temptation and suggest a contemporary parallel situation. Then have the group determine whether and how Jesus' solutions are relevant to us today.

Jesus' temptations give us an interesting insight into Satan's devices. He does not simply attack at our *weaknesses* but, as in Jesus' case, at our *interests* (i.e., Jesus' ministry). Encourage the groups to suggest contemporary situations that test us at our interests—tempting us to do the right thing in the wrong way.

Step Five: Assignment

Read chapter 3 of *Triumph Over Temptation* again.

LESSON SEVEN

Objectives: The group should be able to
1. Explain how the cross was the great testing tree for Jesus.
2. Make a statement of personal faith relative to the cross of Jesus.

Step One: Getting Started

Begin the class with a brainstorming session. Ask the class what kinds of thoughts and emotions must have been going through Jesus' mind the night He prayed in the garden. Let everyone have a chance to suggest ideas, but do not comment on them—good or bad. The purpose of brainstorming is to get a lot of ideas in a free and open atmosphere.

Step Two: Digging Deeper

Divide the class into groups of four to six. Each group will work on the same assignment, but it will be easier in smaller groups. Have the class read Matthew 26:36-46; Mark 14:32-42; Luke 22:39-46. Then ask them to write a synopsis of Jesus' ordeal in the garden in their own words, based on all three Scripture accounts. Have each group select a reporter to read his group's synopsis to the entire class.

Step Three: Discussion
1. Angels came and ministered to Jesus after His temptation in the wilderness (Matthew 4:11). What role, if any, do angels play in our temptations?
2. Why do you suppose Jesus urged His disciples to pray that they would not enter into temptation (Luke 22:40)?
3. Do you think there is any correlation between the disciples' sleeping in the garden—instead of praying—and their desertion when Jesus was arrested? If so, explain.
4. Why was the cross such a "testing" tree for Jesus?
5. Besides the actual fact of the atonement, what does Jesus' victory at His ultimate testing tree do for your own personal faith?

Step Four: Application

The last discussion question should draw out some interesting insights from the students. Some of the following items will probably be answered in that discussion, but this activity will give all the students a chance to apply it to their own situations. Have them complete these statements privately, sharing only if they want to.

1. Because of Jesus' victory at His ultimate testing tree, I am encouraged about my own testing situations. The one that has bothered me most is. . . .

2. Jesus shows me that victory in temptation is sometimes difficult and painful. I've been looking for an easier way out regarding. . . .

3. Jesus' agony in the garden shows me it's not wrong to wrestle with my feelings, as long as I submit them to God's will in the end. The feelings I have been wrestling with most are. . . .

Step Five: Assignment

Read chapter 4 of *Triumph Over Temptation.*

LESSON EIGHT

Objectives: The group should be able to
1. Define Patterson's terms, the "terrible triad" and the "triumphant triad."
2. Cite at least three Scripture passages that link faith, hope, and love.
3. Explain how each part of the "triumphant triad" offers defense against a part of the "terrible triad."

Step One: Getting Started

Write the following Scripture references on small strips of paper, and give one to each of the first six students to arrive:

1 Corinthians 13:13	2 Timothy 1:12-14
1 Thessalonians 5:8	Romans 8:28
Galatians 5:5, 6	Ephesians 3:13-19

Ask these students to read the passages aloud to the group and to make some comment on how the passages relate to temptation.

Step Two: Digging Deeper

Divide the class into three groups. Each group will take one of the three parts of the "triumphant triad," love, faith, and hope, and search for Scriptures that define it, describe it, or relate it to victorious living. Also have them note passages that mention one or more parts of the "terrible triad," the lust of the eyes, the lust of the flesh, and the boastful pride of life. Provide concordances for the class to use.

After a few minutes of research, have each group list and read the Scriptures they have found. Note any passages that contain all three parts of either triad.

Step Three: Discussion
1. How much, in your opinion, does a person's knowledge of God's Word affect his ability to handle temptation? Leader: note Jesus' quotations in the wilderness as well as 1 John 2:14-16.

2. What types of sin can you think of that cannot be classified as lust of the eyes, lust of the flesh, or boastful pride of life? Is 1 John 2:16 intended as a summary of all types of sin?
3. How do you define "sanctification"? How is it related to the "triumphant triad"?
4. Do you think the Father, Son, and Holy Spirit play different roles corresponding to love, faith, and hope? If so, what? If not, why don't you think so?
5. Discuss the diagram on page 59 of *Triumph Over Temptation*. What basic point does it make?

Step Four: Application

This is another matter that should be kept private. Sharing should be strictly voluntary.

First, have each student rate himself in respect to his own personal love, faith, and hope. Use a scale of one to ten on each, ten being the best rating.

Then have them rate themselves in regard to lust of the eyes, lust of the flesh, and boastful pride of life. Again, use a scale of one to ten, ten meaning it is a most troublesome temptation point.

Finally, have them compare the ratings: love against lust of the flesh, faith against lust of the eyes, and hope against the boastful pride of life. Do the high numbers run in pairs? If they do, what should the students do to build up those defensive points of the triad? Have them make specific plans.

If the high numbers are not in pairs, perhaps they have inadequately assessed their strengths and weakness. Is there some secret sin they cannot even admit to themselves? Have they underestimated their own strength in some areas? Or perhaps Satan is working even harder to topple their strongest defenses. (Or, for that matter, Patterson's theory might not be 100% accurate.) At any rate, have the students plan at least one specific action to improve at least one of their ratings.

Step Five: Assignment

Read chapter 4 of *Triumph Over Temptation* again.

LESSON NINE

Objectives: The group should be able to

1. Explain how love defends against the lust of the flesh, how faith defends against the lust of the eyes, and how hope defends against the boastful pride of life.
2. Relate the defense of the "sacred alliance" to contemporary testing situations.

Step One: Getting Started

Display a large copy of the diagram on page 59 of *Triumph Over Temptation* in the front of the classroom. As the students arrive, ask them to write on the chart the name of something that is tempting to people today. These should be written to correspond with the proper heading (Lust of the Flesh, Lust of the Eyes, Boastful Pride of Life). For example, if one writes, "Overeating," he should write it near "Lust of the Flesh." Discuss the activity only briefly. You will come back to it later.

Step Two: Digging Deeper

Divide the class into three groups. Each group will need a dictionary, Bibles, and a group reporter.

Group One will look up the words *lust* and *flesh* and write a definition of *the lust of the flesh*. Then they will look at the Scriptures cited by Patterson under the heading "Love." They are to look for contrasts between their definition and the Scriptures cited: Matthew 22:35-40; Galatians 5:13; 1 Peter 4:8; Ephesians 6:11; Romans 8:35-39.

Group Two will look up the words *lust* and *sight* and write a definition of *the lust of the eyes*. They will look for contrasts between that definition and the Scriptures cited under "Faith": 1 Timothy 6:17-19; Hebrews 11:1; 1 Peter 5:8, 9; James 1:2-4; 2 Corinthians 1:24; Hebrews 10:38, 39; 1 Corinthians 16:13; Romans 5:1-3; 1 John 5:4, 5.

Group Three will look up *boast/boastful* and *pride* and write a definition of *the boastful pride of life*. They will contrast that definition with the following Scriptures: Colossians 1:23; Psalm

78:7; Romans 12:12; Romans 5:2-4; Romans 15:4, 13; Romans 8:24, 25; 1 Thessalonians 1:3; 1 John 3:3, 4; Hebrews 6:18-20; Colossians 1:27; 1 Timothy 1:1; 1 Peter 1:3-5.

After each group has completed its research, the group reporters will report their findings to the class.

Step Three: Discussion

1. "Love covers a multitude of sins" (1 Peter 4:8). Discuss this verse: Whose sins are covered, the lover or the one loved—or both? What does it mean, to "cover" sins? How is this done?
2. Paul said, "We walk by faith, not by sight" (2 Corinthians 5:7). Is faith, then, *blind*? Discuss the basis or reason for our faith.
3. Note how many of the verses cited in this lesson combine two or more of the elements of faith, hope, and love. Is it an oversimplification to divide them up and say each is a different point of defense? Can one work without the others? Discuss how they are different and how they are alike.
4. How are faith, hope, and love related to Christ and the Bible?
5. What is *grace*? What is its role in our defense against temptation?

Step Four: Application

Go back to your three groups. Ask each group to trace a temptation on the chart from Step One as it "attacks" the individual and as he resists it. Group One should choose one from the lust of the flesh, Group Two from the lust of the eyes, and Group Three from the boastful pride of life. Have them note how love, faith, and hope—as well as other virtues—contribute to defeating temptation.

Step Five: Application

Read chapter 5 of *Triumph Over Temptation.*

LESSON TEN

Objectives: The group should be able to

1. Explain the "civil war" within a person when he wants to do right but sins.
2. State the futility in trying to clean up one's life before coming to God.
3. Recite the pieces of the "whole armor of God" (Ephesians 6).

Step One: Getting Started

Call attention to the opening paragraphs of "Victory at the Testing Tree." Patterson uses the picture of a toddler wanting his own way to describe our yielding to temptation. Have the class suggest other pictures to describe how, left to ourselves, we would surely do ourselves harm. (Examples: sheep without a shepherd, a ship without a rudder.)

Step Two: Digging Deeper

Divide the class into two groups. Each group will read Romans 7:18-23. Group One will paraphrase the passage, writing in contemporary English what Paul is saying. Group Two will write and perform a skit. Each member in the cast will represent different aspects of the human mind, such as the will, the intellect, and the emotions. Using a specific moral principle that ought to be obeyed, the group will portray how one who knows and wants to do right may still do wrong.

Step Three: Discussion

1. Patterson expresses the idea that it is impossible to overcome Satan on our own before we come to God. What is the difference between overcoming Satan and repentance?
2. In what way or ways do we make ourselves "gods" when we disregard God's will?
3. Is it possible to wear part of, but not the "whole armor of God"? Why or why not?
4. Discuss the offensive and defensive qualities of each piece of the whole armor of God:

Breastplate
Belt
Sandals
Shield
Helmet
Sword

5. How is "putting on Christ" similar to wearing "the whole armor of God"?
6. How does prayer relate to the Word of God? (Note the specific mention of the Spirit's help in our prayers—Romans 8:26—and of the Spirit's role in producing the Word—2 Timothy 3:16.)

Step Four: Application

Have the class suppose the student Patterson mentioned (the one who wanted to overcome some habits on her own before coming to God) had written to them. Ask each to write a reply, tactfully pointing out the futility of trying to beat Satan alone and expressing God's plan of grace.

Step Five: Assignment

Read chapter 5 of *Triumph Over Temptation* again as well as 1 John 5. Research 1 John 5:8 in at least one commentary.

LESSON ELEVEN

Objectives: The group should be able to suggest explanations of
1. 1 John 5:8.
2. "Sin leading to death" and "sin not leading to death" (1 John 5:16).
3. How "no one who is born of God sins" (1 John 5:18).

Step One: Getting Started

Begin the class by noting Plummer's remark about 1 John 5:8, that it is one of the most perplexing passages in the New Testament. Ask each student in the group to share what he found in researching this verse. Note how similar any explanations are to Patterson's explanation.

Step Two: Digging Deeper

Ask the class to work as pairs to outline 1 John 5. Briefly share the major headings each pair comes up with, but not any sub-points. Then work together to put a title over the entire chapter.

Step Three: Discussion
1. What do you think of Patterson's explanation of 1 John 5:8? What revisions might you make?
2. How can John speak of a "brother" sinning (1 John 5:16) in light of his statement that "no one who is born of God sins" (1 John 5:18)?
3. What does Patterson mean, "It is possible that we may lose some battles with Satan without losing the war"?
4. What is "sin leading to death"?
5. How can you tell if a person has committed "sin leading to death"? How much right do you think humans have to make such a judgment?
6. First John 5:20 makes a good conclusion. Why do you think John added verse 21?

Step Four: Application

Have each student think of individuals who were active in the church one year ago but are inactive now. What efforts were made to return them to active service? What can be done now? Have the students write something they can do to help at least one of them if possible.

Then have the students think of individuals who are still part of the church but whose interest seems to be waning. What is causing the situation—outside enticements? inside dissatisfaction? What can be done to avert total withdrawal? Again, have students attempt to make some specific plans for assisting in the situation.

Step Five: Assignment

Read chapter 6 of *Triumph Over Temptation.*

LESSON TWELVE

Objectives: The group should be able to

1. Explain why we do not ask for temptation.
2. Recall God's promise that no temptation is beyond our ability to overcome.
3. Admit personal responsibility for sin.

Step One: Getting Started

Look at the list of testing trees on page 77 of *Triumph Over Temptation*. Ask the class to think of others they might add. Ask, "Which of these trees stands tallest in your forest of testing trees?" (Be willing to share your own answer to this question, if necessary, to create a more open atmosphere for sharing.) Discuss what makes these trees so ominous.

Step Two: Digging Deeper

Ask the class to assume the role of Christian advice columnists and answer this letter:

Dear Adviser,

I have been studying the Bible, and I've learned that temptation and testing are good for me. James says to "consider it all joy" when I'm tested because it will lead to a completeness in my life (James 1:2-4). So I have decided that I need more testing to make myself complete. I want to ask God for more temptation, but that seems strange. It seems I've heard that it would be wrong to ask that. What should I do?

Signed,
Confused.

Have the class answer the letter, citing as many Scriptures as possible and harmonizing the apparent contradiction between such passages as Psalm 139:23, 24 and Matthew 6:13.

Step Three: Discussion

1. How does knowing we possess the power of God within us (2 Corinthians 4:7) make you feel? How do you feel about temptation in light of that fact?

2. Do you think the writer of Hebrews would accept Patterson's identifying the *discipline* of Hebrews 12:6-11 with *temptation*? Why or why not?
3. We are often tempted in order to make us stronger, but why was Jesus tempted? Do you think God allows some of our temptations for the same reason? Why or why not?
4. In what sense might we say that asking for temptation is tempting God?
5. If God always provides a way of escape (1 Corinthians 10:13), why do we so often not find it? How can we be more aware of that way so that we do find it?

Step Four: Application

"'To err is human' . . . and to blame it on someone else is even more human!" Ask the class to think individually of some of their most recent failures in testing. Whom did they blame? Ask them to write a confession to God of their sin, accepting the blame and listing any lessons they learned from the situation. Reassure the students that the confessions will be kept private.

Step Five: Assignment

Read chapter 6 of *Triumph Over Temptation* again. Briefly review the entire book.

LESSON THIRTEEN

Objectives: The group should be able to
1. Define *humility*.
2. State how Jesus is the "champion" of our faith.
3. Write the most meaningful insights they have gained from this study.

Step One: Getting Started

As the students arrive, give each one a copy of the following agree/disagree statements and ask him to respond.

	Agree	Disagree
1. Humility means refusing to accept any credit for anything.	________	________
2. It is impossible to repent without some measure of humility.	________	________
3. To be humble is to assess oneself by God's standards.	________	________
4. A person who is humble can never say so.	________	________
5. A humble person will never make a good leader.	________	________

Discuss the answers briefly; then work together to write a definition of *humility*.

Step Two: Digging Deeper

Patterson lists several lessons we can learn from Hebrews 12. Supply the class with concordances and topical Bibles, and let them work at finding other Scriptures to support each point. You may want to divide the class into nine groups and have each group work on one point (or three groups, each working on three points).

1. Be conscious of the greats of the past (12:1).
2. Rid yourselves of all encumbrances and run wisely (12:1).
3. Put your difficulties in perspective (12:4).
4. Remember the Fatherhood of God (12:5-11).

5. Have courage! Encourage others (12:12, 13).
6. Run the race of peace and holiness (12:14).
7. Keep up with the grace of God (12:18).
8. Don't get tripped up by the roots of worldliness (12:15).
9. Watch out for the sensual (12:16).

Step Three: Discussion

1. How is it possible that "true freedom is possible for us only as we walk within the limitations of God"?
2. Is Satan's roar really "all bluff"? How dangerous is this "lion"?
3. Patterson says, "We live at a critical moment." What's "critical" about it?
4. In what sense is Jesus the "champion" of our faith?
5. How does helping others help oneself?

Step Four: Application

Ask the class to look briefly at *Triumph Over Temptation*, as well as any notes they've taken and kept since the study began. What was most significant to them? Ask each to write the one most meaningful insight he has gained, and then write what action will be taken because of that insight.